Joke Books

by Judy A. Winter

Consulting Editor: Gail Saunders-Smith, PhD

CAPSTONE PRESS
a capstone imprint

Pebble Books are published by Capstone Press,
151 Good Counsel Drive, P.O. Box 669, Mankato, Minnesota 56002.
www.capstonepub.com

Books published by Capstone Press are manufactured with paper
containing at least 10 percent post-consumer waste.

Library of Congress Cataloging-in-Publication Data
Winter, Judy A., 1952–
Jokes about school / by Judy A. Winter.
    p. cm. — (Pebble Books. Joke books)
Includes bibliographical references.
Summary: "Simple text and photographs present jokes about school"—Provided
by publisher.
  ISBN 978-1-4296-4467-9 (library binding)
1. Schools—Juvenile humor. I. Title. II. Series.
PN6231.S3W56 2011
818'.602—dc22   2010002782

Editorial Credits
Gillia Olson, editor; Ted Williams, designer; Sarah Schuette, studio specialist;
    Marcy Morin, studio scheduler; Eric Manske, production specialist

Photo Credits
All photos by Capstone Studio: Karon Dubke except: Shutterstock: Pal Teravagimov,
10 (mountain), Rossario, 18 (slide), trucic, background (throughout), Ultrashock, 22
(toad)

Note to Parents and Teachers

The Joke Books set supports English language arts standards related
to reading a wide range of print for personal fulfillment. Early readers
may need assistance to read some of the words and to use the Table of
Contents, Read More, and Internet Sites sections of this book.

Printed in the United States of America in North Mankato, Minnesota.
122010   006032R

Table of Contents

Where do people
learn to fight dragons?
In knight school.

Where do you learn
how to meet people?
In Hi school.

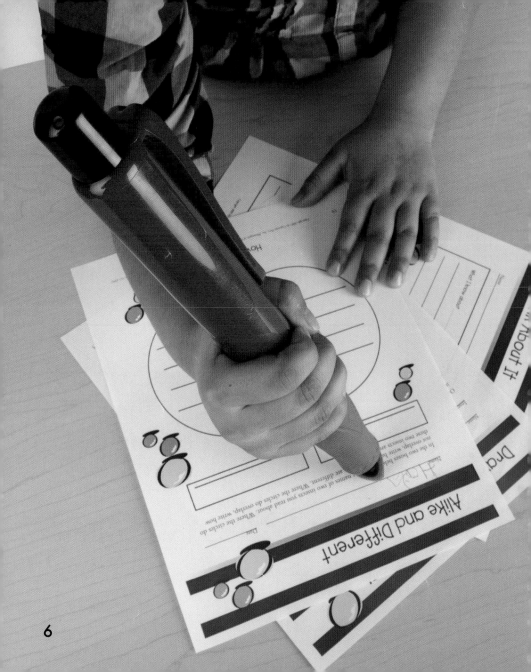

Teacher: Why is your homework in your mom's handwriting?

Student: Because I was using her pen.

Teacher: Did your parents help you with your homework?

Student: No, I got it wrong all by myself.

What is the difference between a teacher and a train?

**One says, "Stop chewing gum."
The other says, "Chew, Chew."**

What do you get if you cross a vampire and a teacher?

A lot of blood tests.

Why did the music student climb the mountain?

To reach the high notes.

Why did the music teacher get locked out of her room?

Her keys were in the piano.

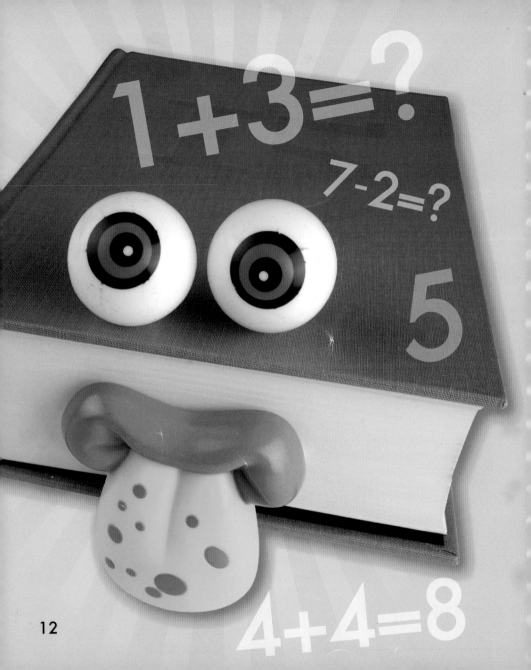

Why was the math book sad?

Because it had too many problems.

Why didn't the two fours want any lunch?

Because they already eight.

What is the king
of the classroom?

The ruler.

Why did Dylan take
a ruler to bed?

**He wanted to see
how long he slept.**

What did one pencil
say to the other pencil?
**You're looking
sharp today.**

What did the pencil say
to the pencil sharpener?
**Stop going in circles and
get to the point.**

Why did the chicken
cross the playground?
To get to the other slide.

What did the girl
say when she walked
into the slide?
Ouch.

Where do library books sleep?

Under their covers.

How do librarians file marshmallows?

By the Gooey Decimal System.

What did the bus driver say to the frog?

Hop on!

How do babies get to school?

The drool bus.

Read More

Harwood, Jerry. *Jokes from the School Bus: Jokes We Thought We Made Up.* New York: Vantage, 2006.

Namm, Diane. *Schooltime Riddles 'N Giggles.* Laugh-a-Long Readers. New York: Sterling, 2008.

Rosenberg, Pam. *School Jokes.* Laughing Matters. Chanhassen, Minn.: Child's World, 2005.

Internet Sites

FactHound offers a safe, fun way to find Internet sites related to this book. All of the sites on FactHound have been researched by our staff.

Here's all you do:

Visit *www.facthound.com*

Type in this code: 9781429644679

Word Count: 265   **Grade:** 1
Early-Intervention Level: 20